Self Portrait in Green

MARIE NDIAYE

Translated by Jordan Stump

Influx Press
London

Published by Influx Press
The Greenhouse
49 Green Lanes, London, N16 9BU
www.influxpress.com / @InfluxPress

Published by Influx Press, London, 2021.
Autoportrait en vert Marie NDiaye, © Mercure de France, 2005
English translation © Jordan Stump, 2014
First English-language edition published by Two Lines
Press, USA, 2014

Printed and bound in the UK by TJ Books.

Paperback ISBN: 9781910312896
Ebook ISBN: 9781910312902

Proofreader: Dan Coxon
Cover design: Carmen R. Balit
Interior design: Vince Haig

DECEMBER 2003 – Evening has come, and the Garonne is rising hour after hour in the dark.

We all know the river can rise nine metres above its banks before it overflows, thanks to the levees surrounding the village.

That much we know. It's the first thing you learn when you make up your mind to settle in this place, eternally under threat from the floodwaters of the Garonne. What we don't know this evening is what's coming tonight, or tomorrow – if, like last time, ten months ago, the water will stop at the top of the levees, or, as it did twenty-two years ago, spill over, submerge the streets, invade the ground floor of the houses, sometimes the second floor, sometimes the whole house.

We can only wait and watch. Once the level nears eight and a half metres, we'll be told to park our various vehicles on the plateau, just outside the next village. That hasn't happened yet.

We can only keep waiting and watching. No sign, for the moment, of the long, slow column of trucks, cars, tractors, campers, and combines rolling through the night, crossing the canal, making for a place the Garonne will never reach.

We wait, we watch. The object of our vigilance is not some Old Man, it's not le Mississippi, it's not le Danube or le Rhône; no one here doubts for a moment that la Garonne's essence is feminine. She's brown tonight, heavy, almost bulging.

2002 – Because it was in front of her house that I saw her each day, for a long time I couldn't distinguish that green presence from her surroundings.

I drove by, taking the children to school, then I drove by again later, now alone, on my way back, then twice more in the evening, going off to pick up the children and bringing them home, and each time, without exactly meaning to, I glanced at that old farmstead's front steps and barren yard, and each time my gaze encountered an undefined form that immediately after melded in my memory with the single tree on the lot, a tall, spreading banana tree.

Four times a day, then, I drove by her house. And I looked at her and didn't see her, and yet a vague unconvinced feeling always turned my head in that direction, though I noticed nothing, ever, but a lovely, surprising banana tree. I stepped on the brake as I drove past, almost at a crawl, and never once did my gaze fail to meet with the still, watchful silhouette of the woman in green standing near the far-more-imposing banana tree, and I know that beyond all possible doubt. Because four times a day my heart was gripped by something unnamable, though not absolutely malign, the moment I passed by the farm with the lone banana tree in its fenced yard, and then afterwards, all along the road to the school, in all sorts of yards, I looked at many, many other banana trees with the most perfect indifference.

But I like knowing names, and, convinced it was not knowing who lived in the farmhouse that was bothering me, I asked around. 'Oh, that place? Those are just the X—s,' people said. And it was a common name in the area, and belonged to many other families besides. There was nothing to be had from a name like that, nothing to learn.

One morning I stop the car in front of the house. I shut off the engine, pull the hand brake, then turn to my four children, three of them in the back seat and the oldest beside me in front. It's a spring morning, warm and glittering. The children's arms and legs are bare. Their hair shines. The windows are rolled down and the car is filled with the smell of honeysuckle, as if we were all wearing perfume. But my children's skin smells naturally of honeysuckle, their necks and their cheeks. I smile at them all with the playful squint that announces I've come up with a new game. They're still small. I whisper:

'Look closely at that banana tree. Is there something or someone anywhere near that banana tree?'

And each of my children looks towards the farmhouse, and their attentiveness, their docility, and their concentration, the utter lack of reserve in their obedience, all that brings me to the verge of tears. It's something else, too. It's also the nearness of that banana tree, of course, with its leaves so broad that any one of them could enfold my youngest child, it's also the imminence of a discovery. A golden dust floats above their heads. Their foreheads are rounded and serene, their napes still pale. Have I mentioned this? My children's arms and legs are bare, because the air is warm, intoxicating.

They were a little disappointed.

'There's nothing at all beside that banana tree,' they whispered.

'Sure?' I asked.

A shiver ran down my back.

'Sure,' said my children, with unmingled certainty.

I turn the key, put the car into gear, and start off a little faster than necessary, not taking a last look back at the farmyard. 'You're the one I need,' I begin to sing under my breath, and when I check the rear-view mirror just to be sure, I can see that my uncalculating, unafraid children are happy, they've already stopped thinking about that big banana tree. They're not thinking about the desolate farmhouse, they're not thinking about what they didn't see near the banana tree. We drive slowly, alone on the little road, in the odorous breath, warmer with each passing moment, of a gigantic mouth. That's how I see all this, but I keep it to myself.

'You're sure?' I asked my children, my spine suddenly cold.

And since my children never delight in deceiving me, how could I not believe them? But at the same time, how could I answer that I myself had just seen, had just for the first time made out, beside that banana tree, a woman in green? How could I tell them I found it hard to believe they hadn't seen that woman in green just as clearly as I could now see her, her who until that morning, I realised, had eluded not my eye but my awareness?

Then I said to myself: that woman in green has always been there. She's there every morning and every afternoon, beneath that banana tree, and she watches us creep past her house, and she sees me looking at her without seeing her.

What I don't know is: is she waiting for me? Does she somehow resent not being seen, does it somehow frighten her, or is that just what she wants?

I realise that my children are still in the first stages of this phenomenon, where I myself was stuck until that radiant spring morning when I first found myself seeing a woman in green in her graceless garden, a garden she seems to occupy only at intervals, when it suits her, a garden whose bleakness and blighted look she's surely not to blame for.

The woman in green is there, every day. Is she still there when I'm not around? I obviously can't question my children about that. Or can I? My children, with their bare legs and perfect arms, are utterly without guile. Anything they believe, anything they sense, they'll tell me.

I pull up in front of the school's lilac. The lilac is covered with little white flowers, and all at once their honeyed scent fills the car. It's almost more than we can withstand. I ask my children if their heads aren't swimming a little, as mine is, and they answer no, and I sense that they don't quite understand the expression 'my head is swimming.' Other children come crowding around the car. Some put their heads through the windows, bringing with them a fresh gust of lilac, and I worry it might nauseate my children. The others' legs and arms are also uncovered, their limbs are plump, their skin packed tight with hard, dense meat. Every one of these children is friends with my own. All smiles and darkly glinting braces, their faces are puffed up with excitement, with joy, with the many anticipations and unexplored wonders of the day just begun. I feel relieved. I look at those children with an affection full of gratitude. I feel relieved, swollen with kindly thoughts. Before my children get out of the car, I put on a sly voice and ask:

'If you see someone whenever you go by his house, does that mean he's there all the time, or only when you go by his house? What do you think?'

My four children sit still for a moment to ponder. Then they shrug apologetically, all together, to signal I've asked them a question they can't possibly answer.

Now they're out in the schoolyard, and my two youngest stand glued to a spot beneath the plum trees, with that wavering look, that vaguely lost, uncertain, disoriented air that often comes over very young children when they suddenly find themselves alone amid shouting and jostling. Seeing that makes me melancholy. I'd like to walk into the schoolyard, take them by the hand, and drive them back home. I can't help thinking it's wrong to desert them like this, but I know that's a wrong, dishonest feeling, I know they know perfectly well that they're not being abandoned, not being consigned to some horrific fate. I remember my own fright when I was their age, I think I can remember that, and that's why a lump comes to my throat when I see such young children alone in a vast, raucous playground. Still, what are they thinking? Are they sure this day will end? That they're not stranded here, alone among dozens of frenetically active bodies, for all eternity? They know, they know. Is that certain?

Then a disturbing memory comes back to me: I remember a woman in green from my grade-school days. Tall, brutal, and heavyset, she promises us all a trip to prison if we eat too slowly, if we dirty our clothes, if we don't raise our eyes to meet hers. Her eyes are green, and she matches them with long checked skirts and turtleneck jumpers. Because of her, a pall of dread hangs over the school. She carries more than one child off towards a dark hallway, proclaiming that prison waits at the far end, and cries of terror resound as that stout woman disappears with her little prisoners clamped beneath her green-sleeved arms. The children are never seen again. They must have been seen again, surely, and yet it seems to me that they never come back, that their two tiny chairs sit empty in the classroom, and that this is the natural way of things, terrible and coherent. They hadn't behaved.

And my two little ones, under the Japanese plums, do they behave?

Now they've all gone inside. The schoolyard is empty, the sweet lilac has numbed me. I must have been one of those children the woman in green carted off down an endless hallway, but fear and the inescapability of the torments to come kept me from crying out. Was I ever seen again? It's true that green can't possibly be the sole colour of cruelty, just as green is by no means inevitably the colour of cruelty, but who can deny that cruelty is particularly given to draping itself in all sorts of greens? Before going on my way, I pull three leaves off the lilac and slip them into the pocket of my shorts. That might come in handy, I tell myself, though for the moment I have no idea what's awaiting me.

All the young women are in shorts, because it's a shimmering spring morning, and in the amber air there's an imperceptible threat of the sweltering summer that will unavoidably follow this season, so mild and at the same time heavy with that warning – it's a wall shining bright white in the blazing sun, for example, or a shadeless gravel courtyard I cross through on my way into the town hall, the baking heat already contained within those four walls enveloping me in a way I've forgotten. All the young women are in shorts and sandals. The sandals' soles smack their heels with a certain resolute gaiety. What makes that sensual? Is it the slightly slack strap that lets the foot slip this way and that, and the heel slap the sole? Or is it the vision of unveiled legs? What makes it sensual, and do the legs have to be beautiful, do they have be lustrous, smooth, and long? Or is the beauty of legs, knees, and ankles superfluous for the burgeoning, in the main street of this drowsy town, of an eroticism still enfeebled by winter? Is all that possible in a town this far removed from the breeziness, the rustle, the hum of the city, is it possible?

All the young women were in shorts, that dazzling morning. Leaving the town hall, I walked with long strides in my army-style khaki shorts, perfectly pleased to be who I was in that place – the main street of a humdrum little town – and at that time, and this contentment was crowned by a vague surprise at the very existence of such a plenitude, the conceivability of such a pleasure. That's when I run into Cristina, but as soon as I see her I'm not sure it's her rather than Marie-Gabrielle or Alison. Not that her name escapes me: it's just that, among those three women, I no longer know which this one is. Deep in my pocket, my fingers squeeze and shred the little lilac leaves. This person who might be Cristina is a young woman, so she's wearing

15

shorts, elastic and clinging, with a print of green flowers against a green background. My elation dwindles a little. It occurs to me that wariness might be called for. And yet I like the idea that soon I'll be driving once more past the house of the woman in green, and she'll be standing there, knowing I'm going to stop. But Cristina's shorts are something else altogether, because I hadn't expected them, and because green isn't the usual colour for women's shorts, in the first days of spring, is it? Cristina keeps her hands behind her, pressed flat against her powerful hindquarters to display her shorts' exuberant colour as flagrantly as she can. She stands with her legs commandingly spread, blocking the entire width of the pavement. As luck would have it, she keeps her sunglasses on, and I've forgotten what her eyes look like, or Marie-Gabrielle's, or Alison's. Her blond hair is pulled into a ponytail so severe that the skin on her temples seems stretched to the splitting point. If this woman really is Cristina, I remember that she's my friend. Cristina has a stronger claim to that title than Marie-Gabrielle or Alison, who are, as best I can recall, nothing more than cheerful companions, in whom one would never think of confiding, because any admission of weakness, of any tiny private anxiety, would be met with frosty disapproval and nothing more. Have I ever revealed anything at all to Cristina? Certainly not, it's not in my nature. But her entire person is awash with sympathy, with understanding just waiting to be called on. I then thought, in a surge of abandon, that the woman in green beside her banana tree might have been waiting for just that: for me to unburden my heart to her.

'Oh, this has never happened to me before,' says Cristina in her hoarse, muffled voice. 'There are two things, and they're both different from each other… The first… you already know… I, you know, I left the kids… for two days, I think… two or three days… with my parents, yes, for a holiday… just a little holiday… at grandma and grandpa's… and… you know my kids, you know them… are they… how can I put this… are they intolerable… coarse… completely disobedient?'

'Not at all,' I say, taken aback.

As I remember, my friend Cristina has no children. In which case, who is this woman?

'No one could say that… call my kids that,' she goes on. 'Oh, they like to run around… they… they're full of energy… like all children… children today… vigorous, healthy…. Anyway, they're out at grandma and grandpa's… at my parents', I mean, and yesterday, Sunday, I go… you understand… I go… get them… pick them up, and I drive up to the house… grandma and grandpa's house… my parents' house… and it was… oh, absolutely silent… just… just the insects cheeping… maybe… absolutely silent… and I tell myself… they're… they're all taking a nap…. I don't want to bother them… so… I don't jiggle the bell… the big metal bell on the gate… so I… I climb over the hedge… a hole… a sort of hole, a low spot… in the hedge… and I climb over it, without making a sound… and I come to… the terrace… and there… I hear… my God, I hear… someone crying… a man crying and I… I look… I look through the glass door and I see… I see my father, grandpa… papa, quietly crying… in front of grandma, my mother… she's standing there, helpless… her arms hanging limp… head down… pitiful, miserable… oh, that's the first time… my father crying... first time I've seen him... anyway... and he's talking... no, he's almost shouting... and my God, he says... he says... and he's talking about my kids, I can tell... his grandchildren... who really aren't all that... right?... About my kids on holiday with them... he says... to my mother... "I can't take them anymore, I can't take them anymore"... and he also... also says... "I'm leaving, I can't stay here, I can't stay in this house with them here"... and he's talking, you understand, about my... about my kids... and I... I left... discreetly... I climbed over the hedge the other way and then... I... I came back... later... and everything was... everything seemed... normal... just two kids on holiday at grandma and grandpa's... and I knew... I knew... that wasn't how it was... wasn't how it really was at all!'

Two tears rolled out from under Cristina's (?) tinted lenses. I wasn't sure what to say. What bond was there between us? And was she not guilty of having such children? Who was she? I really couldn't think what to say. I was looking down at Cristina's thick brown sandals. I took the little bits of lilac leaves from my pocket and carefully crumbled them over her feet.

'The other thing,' says Cristina, 'maybe you've already heard...'

No, I answer playfully, I never hear anything. And since, for anyone who knows me, that's an obvious, barefaced lie, I tell myself that if this woman really is my friend Cristina she'll protest, give me a little swat on the shoulder – but no, she goes on, grim-faced, standing perfectly still.

'A bunch of us saw it, in our yards, on the riverbank, in... Apparently there were even people who saw it in the schoolyard. The mayor... the mayor knows all about it. He saw it too. Something black, and quick. Oh, there were plenty of people who saw it.'

Cristina's words are coming faster now. Her voice is sharper than usual. With a little hop she pulls her legs together and keeps them that way, squeezed tight. I ask:

'What is it? What did it turn out to be?'

'You haven't seen anything?' Cristina asks.

'But what is it?'

'You haven't seen anything?'

All at once she pulls off her sunglasses. And then it's clear, I don't know that face. On the opposite pavement a young woman waves in my direction. It's Cristina, wearing little pink shorts.

'You haven't seen anything?' the first woman says again, and her tone is at once urgent, suspicious, and frightened.

I resolve not to keep this conversation up one moment longer. She vigorously wriggles her right foot, without looking at it or lowering her eyes, to shake off the shredded lilac leaves. Then she shoots me a glance full of unspoken anguish, whirls around, and hurries off, raising little clouds of dust under her sandals.

I'm so rattled I hardly notice Cristina crossing the street in her tiny pink shorts, with her graceful, jaunty gait. She kissed me twice on each cheek and I inhaled her flowery scent. Cristina smelled like a spring flower, a simple white flower. What she then said I'm not sure I can believe myself. Still, I know I didn't imagine it. She really did say it, however unlikely it seems. In a whisper, she said to me:

'A bunch of us saw it, in our yards, on the riverbank, in... Apparently there were even people who saw it in the schoolyard. The mayor... the mayor knows all about it. He saw it too. Something black, and quick. Oh, there were plenty of people who saw it.' What could I have answered, if not:

'But what is it?'

Cristina shrugs, vaguely spreading her arms. Her chin tenses, quivers. Cristina is usually such an impetuous woman that at first I don't grasp the depth of her distress.

'No one knows,' she murmurs.

Cristina is very pretty. Little girls turn and stare when she walks by. I'm proud to have such a charming, vivacious woman as my friend, a woman who can wear a pair of tiny pink shorts with credibility and good humor. I'm grateful to her, because now I recognise her so perfectly. I put one arm around her shoulder to reassure her, I'm not sure about what. Her shoulders sag. She's completely disarmed. Seeing that, I don't press her to tell me anything more.

'The town's sent some workers to go search the school grounds,' Cristina continues. 'I'm on my way there myself. I'm worried.'

Why so worried, I ask myself, since she doesn't have any children? And consequently, I ask myself: did I recognise her as perfectly as I thought?

Once the schoolyard and the little adjoining woods have been fruitlessly searched, I get back in my car and head for our house, a few kilometres from town. It's already near noon. Three hours have gone by since I set off for the school, and I never noticed. Could it be that the woman in green shorts, that stranger I took for Cristina, who must herself have confused me with someone she knew, could that woman really have kept me there talking for two full hours? It doesn't seem likely. Also, I think about that scene she described for me, the weeping father revealing his hatred for his grandchildren, and it seems naggingly close to something I've heard or read before. Either someone once told me about it or it comes from a novel that woman and I both happen to have read. And then she acted it out, while I listened – and I wonder: was I acting too? And did she realise I wasn't? But was she acting herself? There, then, are all the things I don't know. Now I'm in a hurry to get home so I can look through my books and find the one where she might have found that story. For that matter, I could well be mistaken, and that scene is reminding me of another, almost identical, and in that case fictional, while the first is simply drawn from the false Cristina's existence. I know I can't go straight home, and that makes me a little impatient, or maybe apprehensive. It's noon, and the sun is beating down starkly on the water-willow fields. This hot day has left us all a little downhearted, I think, anticipating the summer that's still to come, exhausted in advance.

I park in front of the house with the banana tree. The woman in green is gone now. A shiver of relief, almost triumph, quickly mutes my surprise and disappointment. I tell myself: my children had it exactly right, there never was a...

I get out of the car all the same. I push open the gate and start down the walk. I look up towards the second-floor balcony. The sunlight is dazzling. I shade my eyes with one hand, and that's when I see her, up on the balcony. Then she straddles the railing and throws herself off. I'm very aware of my little smile. Because I'm saying to myself: is all this really real?

A little later I'm sitting in the kitchen of that house I so often passed by, never dreaming I might one day go inside.

The woman in green fell heavily into the tall, green, unmowed grass. Oddly spry, she stood up, patted the dust from her green trousers, brushed off her green T-shirt and black shoulder-length hair with one hand. I walked towards her, thinking: she could have killed herself, she could have hurt herself very badly. I was angry, sure this was all some ridiculous act. But when, one day long after, I remind her how she dropped from the second floor the moment she saw me coming into her yard, when I tell her how irritated and put out that stunt left me, she will solemnly swear that she wasn't jumping to make an impression, that she really was hoping to do away with herself, definitively or otherwise.

She quickly rises to her feet, but now she has a limp. She tries to hide it by walking very slowly, and I conclude she's the cavalier sort. I don't know if I'm supposed to look grave or lighthearted. She tells me to come in for a cup of coffee, even though noon's not ordinarily an hour for offering coffee. All around us, the countryside is perfectly silent.

'You wanted to see me?' she asks, once she's sat down across the table, facing me.

She has very pale green eyes, like the ogress in my school when I was a child. I don't answer her question. We hold our coffee cups with both hands in front of our mouths, and we look at each other over the rims with a hint of suspicion. Truthfulness would require that I tell her, 'I had to make sure you exist.' And since I can't tell her that, I say nothing. She introduces herself, very gracious, obliging, tells me her first name, then her family name, which I already knew.

Her words hang in the air. She's waiting for me to respond in kind, to tell her who I am. Cautiously, I say nothing. In spite of the things surrounding us in this drab kitchen, outfitted in the seventies and never refurbished since, in spite of this woman in green's face so close I could hold out my fingers and touch it, something intangible, a veil, a glimmer of unreality makes me reluctant to tell her who I am. I don't entirely believe in what she is. Not that I think for a moment she's pretending – for one thing, the name she gave me as hers is the very one I'd been told – but I sense that she's taken on the attributes of some other person, and doesn't realise it herself. That's not very clear. I have to explain myself more precisely. I believe that the woman in green, who told me her name was Katia Depetiteville, is not Katia Depetiteville, and I believe that if I asked people in the village for a description of Katia Depetiteville they wouldn't describe this woman, the woman in green. They'd describe a very different person. But the woman in green doesn't know that. She sincerely and naturally believes herself to be Katia Depetiteville. And for what reason? Is it so that, at various moments in my life, I might meet up with a woman in green? Because this is only one among many. In a plaintive, toneless voice, she tells me of the difficulties of her existence in this Aquitaine countryside, the frequent absences of a husband who is furthermore alcoholic and over-talkative, the coldness of her grown-up children, now grasping adults in their faraway towns. Her very green gaze is pale and cold. The hours go by as she speaks, giving up on hearing me say a word. The hours go by, but I don't notice. What exactly she's saying I'll soon have forgotten. I'm wondering: where is the real Katia Depetiteville? When, later, in the village or waiting outside the school, I speak of the woman in green, people will answer, dumbfounded: Katia Depetiteville has been dead for ten years or more. And I won't be surprised, having sensed it in advance.

I want to be away from this house, and the woman in green tries to hold me back. She doesn't lay a hand on me, she only speaks. Another part of me would like to stay a little longer. I'm always interested in stories. Nevertheless, with some effort, I manage to go on my way. From the yard I can hear her still talking in the kitchen, I hear her lazy voice, her droning sentences, her plain words, and I tell myself: lucky for me she's not a gifted speaker.

I'll see her again, we'll be almost friends. I know she'll be replaced one day by another green woman, whom I won't have chosen either.

DECEMBER 2003 – Why, since we take pains to protect our cars, since we devote the necessary time to driving them off someplace where the water can't touch them, why, having done that, do we hurry back to our endangered houses, as if those houses were living beings that we mustn't under any circumstances abandon to the flood? Why, once we've carried the ground-floor furniture upstairs, do we not flee, why do we prefer the prospect of imprisonment in our houses surrounded, if not filled, with cold, silty water, and of a long wait there, stuck on the second floor, idle, bored, and uncomfortable, till the water recedes?

After all, that's how it's meant to be. You don't leave your house. Is it a question of honour? What sort of honour could be involved, when there's nothing to defend, no one to safeguard, and what will the house remember of all this? What gratitude will the house feel at not having been left alone in the churning waters?

For years my father was self-employed as a seedsman, then as a restaurateur. He picked out the restaurant's name on his own. He called it Ledada, he furnished it with garden tables and chairs, painted animal frescoes on the walls in bold, sweeping strokes. He grew out his hair, and dyed it to hide the grey. He remarried, and lost so much weight that he began to look strikingly like photographs of himself as a lanky young man, and that filled him with pride. He hung the most flattering of these photos over the tables at Ledada. When some female customer enquires who that tall, lithe, handsome young man in black and white might be, my father answers in a mysterious voice, 'Oh, that's someone who'll go far.' And then, 'Do you find him attractive?' My father likes to make conquests, and now he can indulge in a gratuitous sort of seduction, unhurried and playful, since he's just remarried. For twenty years his new wife was my best friend. Would she still be today, had she not married my father? Surely she would. She waits tables and takes in the money, and all that would belong to the realm of life at its most banal, in my opinion, were it not for a significant detail that has, ever since she became my stepmother, characterised this woman who was once my friend: she dresses only in green. I believe she had brown eyes. And now, by the grace of contact lenses, those eyes are green. Beaming, she explained that all her life she'd dreamt of having green eyes rather than brown, and she had to wait for a husband with a substantial income before she could dream of fulfilling that desire for permanently green eyes, which cost her no less than five euros a day. I asked my wisp of a father what he thought of this caprice. I wasn't joking. The fact is, I found nothing at all amusing about it. I told myself: here we go again. Again the ambiguity, the groping, the unanswered questions about all this green.

My father sketched delicate circles on the kitchen floor with the tip of his shoe, and I gauged the extravagant length and slenderness his leg had acquired. I sensed his unease.

'And another thing, aren't you overdoing this thinness of yours?' I asked him more gently. 'Couldn't weighing so little be bad for your health?'

'Very possibly,' he said with a quick laugh. 'But, you know,' he went on, 'you can't let yourself go. Look how wiry I am! Fat won't stand a chance with me.'

I returned to the subject at hand:

'You married a brown-eyed woman, and you must have been fond of her eyes. But if they're green, doesn't that change your feelings for her in some way?'

My father went on making his drawings and abstract designs on the floor, looking away, and I understood that his wife's eyes, my ex-best friend's eyes, were a subject he'd sooner steer clear of. My father is on his fifth or sixth marriage. Presumably he doesn't want to take any chances, if he can help it, now that he finds himself aging and tired, and it seems a safe bet that he'd rather avoid speaking words that might be heard or repeated outside the kitchen, with which his wife might one day arm herself to demonstrate that he never loved her. Who am I to go undermining their union's foundation? It simply seems to me that my father – much thinner than before, yes, but no longer young or strong – has failed to appreciate the enormity of those changes in his wife's appearance. He pretends not to see the uniformly almond-green suits, the green cotton tights, the bottle-green lace-up flats. Or else he pretends to believe all this is simply a matter of his wife's personal tastes, on which he prefers to have no opinion, and has no connection

27

with their marriage, or the fact that his wife's stepdaughter was once her best friend. But how, for my part, not to see a meaning in all this, something fated? How not to see, in the apparent coincidence of my father's remarriage and the transformation of my friend into an eternal woman in green, a message intended for me, transmitted not only by that woman's personal colour but by the couple themselves, a green woman and a skeletal father? How to read that message I don't yet know.

Now for an idea of our relationship with each other and the typical atmosphere of Ledada, the restaurant my father opened in the twentieth arrondissement of Paris. At this time, I still have only one child. He's five years old, and we've come to Ledada for lunch, at the invitation of my stepmother. That was something I had to get used to: being invited to visit my own father by my childhood friend, convinced that if I showed up unannounced, if I appeared at the door as if I belonged there, a certain nettled reserve on their part, an exaggerated politeness, would make it clear I'm supposed to avoid any sign of familiarity, which they would find demeaning and upsetting. I sit down with my little boy at the table they've reserved for us. My father and his wife are ceremonious. They move the plastic furniture here and there with a distinguished gravity. Pained, I observe that my stepmother is even heavier than last time, and that my father, ever slighter, must weigh half what she does. Once my friend was a slender girl of her time. Once my father was a robust man, skilled in contact sports. Is it all this green that's undoing them? I wonder, ill at ease in my stepmother's transparent, emerald gaze. My father disappears into his kitchen, then personally brings us the chicken with lime juice or peanut sauce, and although they're both serving us, although the child and I are sitting while the other two bustle around us, we know they're the masters here, the power, the lords of this modest manor, we know it, the child and I, every bit as well as my father and his green wife. They're displaying their enigmatic intimacy for our benefit, and yet our presence here is unnecessary, is in fact invasive. My deep, longstanding friendship with this woman was over as soon as she married my father. I've sometimes told myself this might be for the best. Would it be acceptable for me to hear intimate secrets about my own father? For me to laugh at his behaviour as she and I once laughed together at so many boys? No, that would not be a good thing. And maybe it's also to tell me I'm supposed to keep my distance that my friend has become a woman in green.

One day, one of my father's sons, a man far older than I, bursts into Ledada while I happen to be dining there. He's clutching a golf club with both hands. So he's a golfer, I say to myself, indifferent. Of all my father's children, he's the one I dislike the most. He wordlessly raises the club over his head and smashes it down on the counter. My stepmother stands there, motionless and sedate, coldly observing this unpleasant man's every move. He starts whirling around, brandishing the club before him, mowing down chairs, toppling tables, shattering picture frames. The customers leap up, shout, scatter. My father comes up from the kitchen and stands at the top of the stairs, wrapped in his apron. He looks at his oldest son in silence. He looks at his wife too, but she never so much as glances his way. My father seems

29

abstracted, weary, drained. My stepmother is focused and vigilant. The son drops the club and falls to his knees on the tile floor. His face is wet with tears. He prostrates himself before my father.

'The problem,' I later told my father in Ledada's ravaged dining room, 'is that you have too many children. If every one of your children thinks they have grounds to make you pay for something you've done and maybe forgotten, how can you hope to deal with it?'

'I've never failed anyone,' my father answered.

'That's possible. Nevertheless, you have too many children,' I insisted pointlessly, fully aware of my own bad faith.

Because I feared that my father and the woman in green might have a child of their own, or two, or three, and that this would only compound my father's problems, engulfing all of us, those of his children who feel it in our hearts when some sorrow befalls him. I fear that still, although my friend is no longer a very young woman – does green guard against fertility, I sometimes wonder? No, my friend's not a young woman anymore, and they still haven't reproduced. They've sold Ledada and gone back to the seed shop, raising pigeons in the back room. Little mauve feathers flutter all around my father wherever he goes. That woman in green, my former friend, is the third to come into my life, and to this day, in 2003, she's still there, although I almost never see her, out of indolence and spite. I sometimes ask myself: really, what have you got against her? But is it so vital to ask that question, when the answer is obvious? I can't forgive her for discarding our friendship to take up with my father, a man worn down by too many marriages, too many varied, successive existences, a man who should have elegantly consented to throw in the towel at long last, instead of upsetting the order of the generations, he who had already won so much, and so often. Hard-headed in his emaciation, he'll come to a pitiable end. His daily rations are those of a child of two. Meanwhile, his wife balloons year after year, to the point that she now has her green dresses hand-sewn, because she can't find her size in the shops. All the same, there's no denying it, they exude conjugal bliss. Making them enviable, in the end, in their way – yes, are they not to be envied?

DECEMBER 2003 – After the uncertain night, day broke bright and mild. Nothing the Garonne has in store seems too worrisome when the air is blue-tinged and luminous. Several roads around the village are cut off. At eight o'clock the firemen's siren in La Réole sounds, and that siren, meant to inform us of nothing other than the rise of the water, sends more than one of us into a panic, as we don't understand what it means. We don't know, we've forgotten, how to interpret it: are we supposed to count the blasts from the beginning, and thus understand that the Garonne has hit ten metres at La Réole (which, for us, means disaster, a catastrophic flood in the offing), or do we count only the short blasts that come after one very long blast, which serves solely as an overture for the counting? We don't know. A variety of opinions are voiced, in tones sharpened by anxiety. Why do so many men and so few women enjoy this tense atmosphere, this prelude to valour, to heroism? Why do so many women, who've been living here forever, aspire only to move to a safe place at last, and so few men? Why do the men say, in spite of the

33

extra work, the exhaustion, the apprehension caused by the threat of a flood, and then sometimes by the flood itself, why do they say, without explanation, 'I'll never leave!'? Why should they see leaving as a sign of failure, when there's no point in staying?

2000 – I never met this other woman in green, the fourth or fifth, whose presence in my personal legends eclipses, by its incandescence, some of her more irrefutably real neighbours. I'm not even sure she's actually a woman dressed in green. In the end, it makes little difference. She remains a pure emblem of a green woman, no matter what. Everything I know of her comes to me from Jenny.

A time came when Jenny found herself at a dead end. She was a little less than fifty years old, and everything that had once been hers, everything she'd worked so hard to succeed at, everything she'd devotedly loved had all flitted away in the space of a year. Her adopted son was wandering the world and refused to see her, her husband had left her, she'd just been laid off. Everything had vanished. She's a passive and trusting person, and nothing she'd done was really to blame for this ruination. It had simply happened, beside her, without her realising, and when she woke up it was too late to hope she might recover what was lost.

When I met her she was tall and thin. She wore her hair in a loose bun, and that hair was artificially of the palest blond. Is hair colour a reflection of some moral quality, of goodness and innocence, of those virtues' opposite? Obviously not. The pallor of Jenny's hair in no way expressed what she was.

Nevertheless, even mired in distress, incomprehension, the terror of poverty, she went on carefully bleaching her hair, and gathering it up with just the degree of slackness she liked, so that every day two or three strands would come loose and fall over her cheeks, allowing her, always with the same slow, reflective gesture, unsullied by coquetry or ostentation, to tuck them back behind her ear. She was never concerned about knowing exactly what she looked like. As an image of her self, she wanted to know only the timeless harmony of that minuscule gesture, only the beauty of two fingers lifting up a lock of almost white hair.

11 MARCH , 2001 – Jenny is moving back in with her parents, in the country, since she can't pay her rent. They greet her in pained, awkward silence. They can scarcely believe she has failed so utterly, she whom they were once so intimidated to visit, fearing they might not measure up to her prosperity. She knows what they're wondering, bewildered but severe: does our daughter still have some scrap of dignity left? They allow the first name of the adopted son, their only grandchild, to escape their pinched, pursed lips, and then all of a sudden they're heaving with sobs. Jenny says nothing: what is there to say, she thinks, in the face of this disaster? Is it a disaster? Or only life? Before her hiccupping old parents, before her old parents who've never been very tender or very clement, or benevolent or, in any way, very tolerant, a sort of serenity descends over her. Nothing sadder can happen to the three of them than this: two stiff, prickly old people weeping before their careworn daughter, weeping

because a man who is their grandchild, although he was born to an unknown woman in a place so far away they'll never go there, has decided to have nothing more to do with them, because he despises and hates them. That man used to be a very little boy, who loved his holidays in this countryside, who hopped and rolled around the yard, who considered this yard his own, without qualm or reserve, and now he's fled, burning behind him what he once seemed to love, now he's become a faithless and mysterious person, someone you no longer know, but who seems to know you so well that he refuses to put up with you any longer. Jenny raises her eyes to the austere little house, the grey skies, then looks back down at her parents' tear-streaked faces, and something like an understanding of what the son must be feeling runs fleetingly through her. She knows all this far too well, she tells herself. These poor damp-eyed people are her family. That fills her with a sort of disgust, an impotent exasperation. She'd like these people, who are undeniably her family, and who look on her in the same way, to evaporate by some miracle, without awareness or pain, and leave her alone, and free of any such bond.

20 MARCH, 2001 – Sorrow and bad luck protect her, in a sense. I go and see her at her parents', in that damp, desolate countryside, and I notice they dare make no demands on her, despite their authoritarian ways. She's kind and gentle and so bleached as to not seem real. The sight of my children is painful to her. It was a cruel mistake to bring them. In hopes of warding off who knows what disasters, she continually lifts one hand to her hair, the gesture now spasmodic and unthinking. In spite of it all, in spite of the pain, the shrinking prospects, I tell myself: Oh, she'll come through this all right.

29 MARCH, 2001 – Out for a walk, she happened to run into Ivan, and since Ivan and Jenny had had a love affair in the distant days when Jenny still lived in this countryside, now Jenny suddenly finds herself sitting at Ivan and Ivan's wife's table, now she's been invited to share their lunch, in

the company of several hearty young men, young adults bursting with health and beauty, who are their sons, and now Jenny's feeling dazed in the midst of this whole and resplendent family, now she's wondering if she's not at this moment in her own private dream, witnessing the wonderful life she could have led had she stayed in her parents' village. Because if she had, Jenny doesn't doubt for a moment, she would surely have lived with Ivan, and, remembering her very deep love for him and his passion for her, she shivers with a newborn pain, another pain atop all the sorrows already besetting her, along with a fresh sort of perplexity as it suddenly strikes her as unthinkable that she, Jenny, should find herself in the woeful situation that she does in fact seem to be in, her, Jenny, whom fortune had graced with gifts and skills, she who had always enjoyed such an abundance of choices.

Ivan is sitting across the table from her, and Jenny conceals her lostness behind a pathetic smile, all the while thinking: How he's aged. And she knows perfectly well that he's looking at her and thinking: How she's aged. And then, Jenny tells herself, Ivan can look at the boys that surround them, who are the picture of perfectly successful human beings, and muse that it's worth growing older to revel in that perfection, that success; but for Jenny, where can she look to find this delight in growing older? Where can she look?

30 MARCH, 2001 – On the telephone, she tells me at some length that her love affair with Ivan lasted several years before she decided to leave the province, and in spite of the distance between us I can picture her hard face and clenched

jaw, because I hear a cold, brittle voice that isn't usually Jenny's, a voice she's forcing herself to adopt, I think, so as to keep sentimentality at bay. Jenny is not a sentimental woman. Isn't it a sign of contemptible self-indulgence, Jenny's thinking, to be caught up in a romanticism you never felt when you were young, simply because you have too much time on your hands, and because, in any event, giving into that romanticism now poses no threat, since everything that matters in life lies well behind you? Certainly, Jenny is thinking, belated romanticism is pitiful, pathetic, mediocre. But how to fight it off ? Jenny doesn't ask me, but I can't help inwardly posing that question for her: how to fight it off, yes, how to remain sincerely cold and detached, when as it happens Ivan's face is now never far from her thoughts, and not Ivan's face when he was young and in love with her but Ivan's face today, creased, placid, and a little weary? How to remain hard, clear-headed, and slightly sardonic when Ivan's face, which she sees the moment she wakes up and then sees all day long, always appears to her surrounded by the friendly faces of the wife and sons, who inspire in her no trace of jealousy but only a powerful affection and interest, not lessened but heightened by her melancholy? How to fight it off, in the face of such a melancholy? Against melancholy, against regret, common sense and cynicism can do nothing. She regrets not what was, but what should have been, could have been, had she only made some other choice way back then, and she regrets the choice she made, the path of sorrow. Of course, she says nothing of all this. I can feel it from the forced hardness in her voice.

4 APRIL, 2001 – Now, and only now, I realise that Ivan's wife is a woman in green. I went back to see Jenny, and while her very amenable parents entertained my children, with that cheerful bonhomie, that ability to find fun in nothing at all that the sternest educators sometimes acquire in their old age (rankling Jenny, who observes: 'They were nothing like that when I was little' – but then it was simply impossible for them to be other than they were, because they couldn't imagine children might be treated in any but the most dramatic and intransigent way), while Jenny's parents looked after my children, suddenly seeming to believe that their daughter's troubles in no way forbade them from offering their faces to the first sunshine of spring, in no way forbade them even from forgetting that they had a daughter in difficulty, I went with Jenny for a little stroll in the direction of Ivan's house, because she wanted me to get a glimpse of them, him and his wife. She described the way Ivan drags greedily on a cigarette, how he closes his eyes and then half opens them to blow out the smoke in little puffs, like sighs,

disillusioned; whereas, she told me, Ivan's wife holds her cigarette at her side, between two delicate fingers, all the while cooking with the other hand. Jenny tells me, I think, that this woman always appears in green – I think she tells me that, and now I don't want to question her to make sure, for fear I might learn otherwise. Why do I not want to learn otherwise? There's something dishonourable in that, since as I perceive her Ivan's wife has no need of a costume to be a woman in green. All the same, Jenny did tell me this woman never let herself be seen in any other colour; and this, like her way of just barely clasping her cigarette, her hand close by her hip, forms, along with a welter of similar details, the substance of the charm she exerts on Jenny.

8 APRIL, 2001 – Increasingly, though, it's Jenny and not me who has problems, I'm the one who calls Jenny, simply for the pleasure of hearing her speak. She goes to Ivan and his wife's house every morning, when Ivan's away, in what seems an implicit agreement between the two women. The wife lights a cigarette in front of Jenny, who, never having smoked in her life, having always looked on cigarettes with virtuous horror, can't imagine that pleasure, and yet now she envies this gesture, and her own, her adorable way of pushing a lock of hair back along one side of her head, now strikes her as trivial, inadequate. Her parents' fears have come true: she's losing a part of her dignity, but not for the reasons nor in the circumstances they imagine. She's forgotten that she's a woman adrift, alone and abandoned, that no one anywhere feels any need for her, that she was loyal to her profession

and that her profession coldly rejected her – all that, which so consumes the two old people's thoughts, she's forgotten, and so she's no longer ashamed. But before Ivan's wife she's tormented by the sort of disdain that she feels for herself, for her physical person, her own insignificance. The woman in green humbles her, not deliberately, unaware that she's doing it – and if she did know it and want it, Jenny would never let it happen.

10 APRIL, 2001 – Repeatedly questioned, with no attempt on my part to conceal my burning curiosity, Jenny revealed what the two of them discuss in her daily visits. Ivan's wife does the talking. She lights a first cigarette, silently and slowly, sits down in an armchair, crosses her legs, and, with her cigarette always about to slip from between her index and middle fingers, tells Jenny of the life Jenny would have lived had she spent it with Ivan, her first, overpowering love. Surprised, I ask: 'But what does she know about that?' And Jenny answers that Ivan's wife describes her own life with Ivan, which is a fairly reliable way, thinks Jenny, of showing her the life Jenny and Ivan would have had together. That's what goes on every morning: the one speaks and the other listens, and as the one talks the other feels herself growing small, transparent, and empty, more convinced than ever of her insipidity. In parallel, her regrets about Ivan grow ever more wrenching. I ask, surprised:

'But what's in it for her? Why should she do that?'
And Jenny answers, surprised at my surprise:
'To console me.'

43

I ask:

'Console you for what?'

'For the tragic mistake I made, not choosing Ivan when I still could,' answers Jenny in her hard voice, intended to repel any reaction of pity.

Nevertheless, it seems to me that Jenny comes away from these conversations not consoled but crushed by despair and self-loathing. In a murmur, she tells me:

'We'll never be young again, never.'

I want to object, I want to shoot back: Well, I'm young. I'm only in my thirties, after all. But isn't Jenny right? Oh yes, I tell myself, Jenny's right, Jenny's right. What she's thinking of – the belief in the infinity of possibilities, the illusion that you can forever start over again, that every mark made on you lasts a little while then ends up disappearing – all that we no longer have. I ask Jenny:

'We no longer have that, but isn't it better this way? Isn't it a thing to be grateful for, every day?'

11 APRIL, 2001 – Around eleven this morning, Jenny went to Ivan's wife's house.

The air is mild and perfumed and full of hope. Jenny's blond-white ponytail undulates against her back. Jenny walks with her head high, and she promises herself, although the promise brings a lump to her throat, that this is her very last visit. The time has come to put an end to these lamentations, Jenny tells herself, and to this homesickness, home being the life she never had, with Ivan. That's how she sees this: a land whose soil she trod for a few happy steps, and which she then thoughtlessly left behind, and now it's been wiped off the map. She can never come back. That's the form of her sorrow, of the thing weighing on her heart ever since she saw Ivan again.

The house seems to be empty. Jenny knocks, waits and waits, then goes in all the same. The kitchen and living room sit frozen in an atypical tidiness. She hesitates, sits down. She takes the wife's pack of cigarettes from the little table. She hesitates again, then pulls one out and lights it somewhat clumsily with the lighter she knows so well, which she's found lying on the table like a thing not so much put down as put away. She crosses her legs and smokes. She's aware of her flushed face, her shame. She imagines her parents, eyeing her sternly, reproaching her for being a woman and smoking, for being worthless and smoking.

And then she suddenly stands up and bolts down to the basement, still holding the cigarette. Her shoes clap sharply against the cement steps. In her haste, she almost trips, almost tumbles headlong down the stairway.

She embraces Ivan's wife's thighs and hips. The wife is wearing green corduroy trousers and a blouse of green satin. Her feet are bare, and Jenny notes their soles, grey with dust.

What's left of the cigarette is still clasped between Jenny's lips. She'd like to wash off those feet, already cold, rub them, implore them. Straining to hoist up the body so she can loosen the knot on the rope, she spits out her cigarette butt, then presses her face into Ivan's wife's bulging belly and begins to sob in horror and dismay, now and then shouting out towards the basement walls, which bounce her cry back to her in a feeble echo. The house is deserted, she can call out all she likes – who will hear her?

Two years go by with no news from Jenny, each of us keeping our distance from the other, her, ashamed of confiding in me when it's not in her nature, me, remorseful for pushing her to tell me what she'd rather have told no one.

In a pedestrian street of a small city, one crowded and tiresomely bustling Saturday in the year 2003, I run into Jenny, who, ever the same, pushes back a few strands of hair that have come out of her bun before giving me a kiss. In our joy at seeing each other again, our cheekbones bump painfully. I have on my chest a baby Jenny's never met, of whose very birth she knew nothing. She looks at the baby with delight, and the change makes me realise how downcast and defeated her whole manner had been just a moment before. She points towards the back of the man who was with her, now silently plodding away, hands in his pockets, shoulders slumped. His head is bald, ringed with a crown of grey hairs.

'That's my husband Ivan,' says Jenny, with a faint grimace.

And then a sadness, a bitterness takes shape between us.

Once she's divorced Ivan, once she has, for the second time, moved back in with her parents, who, aneasthetised by so many failures, have finally sunk into a sort of merciful torpor, Jenny summons herself up from my memory and rather grandly invites me to come see them. I find her irritable with the old couple, haughty and curt, as if for some reason they owed her. Gone is the sweetness in her features, gone her appealing look of dismay, replaced by a mask of sarcasm and scorn. The parents serve us the meal they've prepared, Jenny finds fault and complains, and in the end I leave the table to join the two old people in the kitchen, where they're eating their dinner. I sit down beside them to finish my plate. They smile beatifically, unable to understand that they're being mistreated. They've changed in a most surprising way. I know that in another time they inflicted a brutal upbringing on Jenny. After coffee, I want to leave right away, but Jenny recovers some of her warmth and her smiles, and asks me to stay. But when I suggest a walk around the village, her entire face turns cold and hard, and she refuses without the tiniest trace of friendship in her voice.

'She's afraid of that woman,' the mother murmurs to me in an aside.

'That woman?'

'The one who hanged herself.'

Her voice is almost inaudible, a peep. She's terrified.

Jenny has taken refuge in her old-fashioned little room, a girl's room, crouching on her bed, her chin on her knees. I then picture us, four people feeling only the most tangled sentiments for each other, isolated in this grey house in the outer reaches of a gloomy province, and I have only one desire: to run away as fast as I can and desert these three people, whom I promise myself I will never see again.

'I met Ivan's wife,' says Jenny – neglecting to mention that she too was, for one short year, Ivan's wife.

A scowl flashes across my face. Jenny nods vigorously. In a monotone, speaking fast to stave off interruptions, she tells me how she and Ivan, early in their marriage, as they wandered the aisles of a department store, almost collided with a woman draped in a very elegant green coat, with genuine fur collar and cuffs, dyed green. It was her, Ivan's wife, who'd hanged herself to death in her basement, later to be found by Jenny. So it really was her? I smile my disapproval and say nothing.

'It's hard to believe,' says Jenny, 'but I only mention it because Ivan recognised her himself. Ivan's a down-to-earth man.'

And so Ivan, having recognised her, called out her name. And the woman, coolly, as was her way, spoke exactly this sentence:

'So, you two, how's it going?'

Jenny asks me: would a stranger they'd mistaken for Ivan's wife have spoken to them like that?

No, a stranger they'd confused with Ivan's wife would not have spoken to them like that, certainly not. This woman then went on:

'Didn't take you long… I'm doing fine, myself.'

And in fact the only notable difference between this woman in green and the one they used to know lay in this one's greater beauty, but it was still the same beauty, only expanded, vibrant, thanks to contentment, to money, to sexual satisfaction.

'Yes,' Jenny says gravely, 'sexual pleasure most of all, it was perfectly clear in her eyes, in her smile, in her way of rubbing the fur collar against her chin. Ivan saw it just like I did. That was the thing he couldn't get over.'

Then I begin to hop from one foot to the other, staring at Jenny with a gaze drained of tenderness. I ask:

'What couldn't that imbecile Ivan get over? His wife's death? Her reappearance as a contented mistress? Yes, just what was it Ivan couldn't get over?'

Jenny's lips are quivering. How worn she seems, assailed by disillusionment, by multiple losses, by ridiculous, terrifying convictions!

In a tiny little voice she tells me Ivan continually tortured himself after this meeting, belittling himself, desperately jealous of the happiness he thought he saw radiating from his first wife's entire magnificent person. I then understand that what particularly consumed them wasn't seeing a dead woman before them and hearing her speak, but finding her so exultant, so infinitely appealing.

I feel deeply displeased by this nonsense, and I'm not far from hating Jenny, from finding her stupid and mediocre. Adopting a sly, mischievous air, she tells me that Ivan never found the woman in green again, although he took great pains to do so, whereas Jenny met up with her several more times. She saw her in that same department store, in the perfume aisle, then in the park of a nearby city where Jenny worked for a while. The woman recognised her and stopped to talk, still wrapped in her silky coat, gracious and aglow.

In spite of myself, I ask:

'Did you tell Ivan?'

Yes, Jenny told Ivan, and no doubt she was wrong not to conceal her joy and her pride, because it was against her, Jenny, that Ivan's jealousy then turned. Jenny tells me he accused her of conspiring with the other woman. Oh, she couldn't find the words to defend herself.

Did she feel like she was conspiring? Now I can't stop questioning Jenny, I who, so full of disdain, wanted to flee and hear no more of this foolishness. Did she conspire against Ivan? Jenny tells me she never conspired – why would she have conspired? What would she have got, in the way of satisfaction or material goods, from conspiring? But with that their marriage came to an end, both of them fixated on the same person, though in different ways – Jenny longing for nothing less than to strike up a fresh friendship with the woman in green, in the hopes that she might learn about life, might learn everything that's eluded her for the past fifty years, things others know but can't tell her, not knowing just what they might be, and so, thinks Jenny, she might finally understand why everyone who comes close to her ends up turning away in anger and disappointment; and Ivan, for his part, wanting very simply to know how his first wife found her way to such radiance, once delivered of those nearest her. They've separated, but they keep an anxious watch on each other. Jenny says to me, spitefully:

'If she tried to hang herself so she wouldn't have to see Ivan again, do you really think she'd come visit him now?'

And you, I say to myself, poor Jenny, why should she come visit you?

Jenny's mother later confides to me that the hanged woman recently knocked on her door. Jenny's mother opened it, recognised Ivan's first wife, and fainted dead away. She tells me the woman was very beautiful, lovelier and more luminous than before, and she smiled with great kindness and self-confidence.

'She did die, though,' I say.

'Well, now we're not so sure,' the old woman answers.

'It should be possible to find out.'

But the three sons want no part of it. None of them ever spotted their mother again after they saw her lying in her coffin.

'They resent Ivan and me for seeing her,' Jenny says, 'and for not keeping it secret.'

Could it really be that some other woman was buried in the place of the woman in green? But who, in that case, was the hanged woman whose legs Jenny had clasped in her arms? And how could such a misunderstanding arise? I say goodbye to Jenny and her parents, fuming, vowing to have no more to do with this disastrous family. Not yet out of the house, I can already hear Jenny bitterly upbraiding the old couple. They don't say a word, they seem to be listening to her with sorrow and interest.

That was the last time I saw Jenny, and I don't believe I'll be seeing her again, since she's dead. Her parents wrote to tell me they'd found her lifeless in the bed she slept in as a girl. Evidently she killed herself with an overdose of prescription drugs, but her parents didn't say if it was a mistake or a deliberate act, and I myself have no idea. Am I overinterpreting certain turns of phrase, certain wordings, or is there really relief in the old couple's tone, in their way of saying, for example, 'So that's that'? Granted, Jenny had done everything in her power to tyrannise them, after exhausting and defeating them with her many failures.

*

I stopped off to say hello to them, one day when I happened to be driving past their house, not sure why I was taking the trouble, why I should go to such lengths. No, the fact is I didn't happen to be driving by their house, absolutely not. I had to make a sizable detour to get there. It was the middle of summer, and I'd never come there before at that time of year, so I nearly didn't recognise the place, once so dreary, now heavy with ivy and honeysuckle. Ruddy and round in their light summer clothes, Jenny's parents welcomed me almost jovially. They were drinking coffee on the flower-bedecked terrace, in the company of a tall brunette woman with dark green eyes. She was about the age Jenny would have been, around fifty-three, and wearing a short, straight dress with little green and white checks. The two old people were happy, even jolly, joking. I shouldn't have come, I told myself, deflated by the prospect of having to meet someone new, and because the parents clearly had no need of my compassion.

'Well now,' the old woman said to me, 'this is Ivan's wife.'

And I ask:

'So Ivan's remarried?'

She doesn't answer. She pinches her upper lip between thumb and index finger and tugs it right and left, a gesture I remember as her way of expressing unease.

I never saw those two old people and that green-eyed woman again.

How strange it is, after you've spent some forty years alongside your own mother, after you've butted heads with her on all manner of questions but most often and most violently on the inertia, the greyness, the deadly smallness of her existence, which, no doubt wrongly, you thought darkened and depersonalised your own, how strange it is that this woman you can no longer bear to know so well should suddenly metamorphose on her own into a green woman, and one of that type's most alien and troubling forms. In the year 2000, my mother was forty-five years old and living with my two twenty-year-old sisters in a grim, well-kept suburb that she never left, because she worked there as well, in the neighbourhood school. And that's all there was to her life in those days, a round little woman, virtuous, unfailingly solemn, trotting along towards her workplace each morning, never glancing left or right for fear she might glimpse something that looks vaguely or unmistakably like adventure or novelty, for fear she might glimpse a bit of the face of someone she knew, someone she couldn't deny not knowing, who might tell her some troubling story, might reveal some intimate secret. She covered her hair with a dark grey shawl, which also enveloped her cheeks, her chin, her shoulders and chest. She had a proud, almost swaggering ugliness – such, then, was my mother at age forty-five, and such had she been for a very long time, ever since my father left her, her and my sisters, to take up with my childhood friend, ever since she'd resolved, so it seemed, to confront my father's juvenile arrogance with a kind of saintliness, with an equally arrogant withdrawal from the world. I went to see them only rarely, and then I stopped altogether, convinced that my visits were disagreeable for all three of them, forcing them to play host – to make tea and ladyfingers, to chat, to make a fuss over some child of mine, facing the ever-present danger of a question they might find deeply upsetting, however harmless it might seem to me. Two years went by, then, without my seeing or hearing of them. Were my sisters in school, had they married? I had no idea, and little by little I forgot those two sisters of mine. I heard stories of one's addiction to drugs, of the other's alcoholism. Nevertheless, uncertain that these stories did indeed involve my two sisters, I paid them little mind. Besides, I said to myself, suppose it's so? Is it my affair to keep watch over my sisters, look after them, show them affection? No, that is not my affair. Raised in an ambience of confrontation, jealousy, and acrimony, we can't wipe that vitriol from our memories and love each other, even now that we're adults. We can meet and be cordial, but we certainly can't love each other. And so two years went by, in distance and indifference. Inevitably, I thought, something must have come along and altered my sisters' existence, for, although unnaturally faint-hearted, they were still young enough that any trivial decision about their future would bring with it a change, however miniscule, in their fanatical routine. That my mother's life might have strayed from its course, on the other hand, I never once dreamed – because how can you even die, simply that, when you live a life of stone, unchanging and immobile?

In late 2002, pregnant with my fifth child, my thoughts full of the stories told to me by my new friend Katia Depetiteville, or the woman who takes herself for Katia Depetiteville, I receive a postcard from Marseille signed 'Maman'. I first assume there's been some sort of mistake, but the card is indeed addressed to me. Next to the stamp is another stamp, a mock stamp with a tiny photograph of a baby, and an arrow pointing to that baby with the scrawled words: 'Your new little sister.' This leaves me stunned to the point of terror. Without a word to anyone, I bury the card in our neighbour's chicken pen, close by our house. But Christmas is coming, and remorse gnaws at me. If this is all real, I tell myself, my mother deserves an answer. But what if it isn't? Is there no danger in behaving as though it were? One evening when the moon is round, I straddle the chicken pen's fence and dig up the card, just long enough to note the address my mother has written down as her own, then bury it again, deeper. On the other side of the pen, the geese have spotted me, and now, frightened, they're squawking in their horrible, broken, strident voices. I flee, not certain I haven't been seen. Suppose they'd released the dogs, convinced there was a thief on the prowl?

I write my mother a dishonest, overjoyed letter, and, pretending to believe her, offer my delighted congratulations.

She answers immediately with an invitation to come see
her in Marseille. Not one word on my own children, on the
health of this child or that – the one soon to be born she
knows nothing about. I recognise my mother's handwriting:
the dots on the i's are oversized circles, every sentence
contains several startling mistakes, signature mistakes in a
way, unique. She suggests, almost demands, that I come see
them for Christmas, claiming she'll be leaving immediately
after to visit her husband's family. Radically incompatible
with my mother, that word husband leaves me distraught.
The squat woman with the grey edge of a shawl always
encircling her face, the woman with the hollow, yellow
cheeks, with the thick glasses in black plastic frames, the
desperate, inflexible woman who never spoke the name of
any man after my father left, how can that deeply isolated
woman now speak of a husband? And a child? I calculate her
age: forty-seven. Possible, perhaps, but not at all plausible.
And isn't it unseemly to invite me down for Christmas, me
alone, without a word concerning her grandchildren, as if
she suddenly had none, or didn't recognise them?

Two days before Christmas, I'm on my way to Marseille.
We've agreed that my mother will come and meet me at
the Saint-Charles station, and as I wait on the platform,
burdened, anguished, drained, thinking she's forgotten
to come, or that this whole affair is so unlikely that it
can't possibly culminate in the actual arrival of my actual
mother, I see a smiling woman approaching, wearing my
mother's unattractive glasses, followed by a man – and, on
that man's arm, a little girl. The woman is bare-headed, and
her hair is dyed red and cut short, her brow draped with
bangs that she regularly tosses out of her eyes with a jerk of

the head. Her make-up is impeccable, very ladylike, she has fine hose, high-heeled strapped shoes, etc. I stare mutely, knowing it's her, my mother, but unable to feel it in anything about her. She's tall, poised, and, for what she is, perfect. She kisses me politely, without tenderness, and I note that her manners too, and her gestures, are more elegant than before. She introduces the little girl, whose name is Bella, and the father, a certain Rocco. Nothing leads me to believe that she finds this situation at all odd or disconcerting, since she speaks to me as naturally as can be, in that metallic voice that was even long ago hers. She smiles continually, her wide smile without warmth, perfectly at ease, a woman of the world. I fleetingly sense that my mother's gaze is not in unison with her smile, that behind her slightly distorting lenses an anxiety hovers, even a panic, unbeknownst to her. But is that certain? A second later her gaze is bright and joyous. Is that certain?

And so I follow this new little family out of the station, then into a complication of narrow streets, dark despite the blue sky and the bright winter sun. My mother and Rocco walk a few paces ahead, and every so often the child turns around, perched on her father's shoulders, to look at me with an astonishment full of suspicion. She's a pretty little girl, her eyes dark and hard, elegantly garbed in an orange corduroy coat with big brass buttons. Not once do my mother or her husband look back to be sure they haven't lost me. Rocco is much younger than my mother – yet who could ever guess my mother's age now? Rocco must be about as old as I am. And suddenly I discover, as I consider her briskly swaying hips, her delicate calves swathed in shimmering hose, that my mother is a kind of green woman

59

I haven't yet come across – and what fate is it, I wonder, that demands that my mother herself must now cross my path as a green woman, to convince me that such is my destiny? No need to see her actually dressed in green – we're well past such childishness now, in a way. She's dressed in pink, in a suit cut from an inexpensive fabric that manages to put up a good front all the same.

We turn into a dank alleyway, so macerated in its own damp that you can easily conclude the sunlight never touches it. Rocco opens a door and we walk down a dark hallway, where a second door gives onto a room shrouded in semi-darkness. My mother hurries to open the curtains, but the room is scarcely lighter than before. It's small and cluttered, thick with the odours of a stingy, shabby existence. Rocco kindly offers me a sandwich and something to drink. Meanwhile, still standing, one foot perpendicular to the other, my mother looks as though she's struggling to keep the alarm and embarrassment out of her gaze. Whenever she lets down her guard, I see her eyes darting uneasily this way and that, never looking straight ahead. She then raises her hands to take off her shawl, forgetting she's not wearing one. Seeing that I've seen her, she furrows her brow.

I spend three days in Marseille. With each passing hour I am more resolved never to come here again, never to have anything more to do with my mother's new family. She struggles valiantly to bring order to this new life of hers, but the forces at work overrun her on all sides. Little Bella is prone to tantrums of paroxysmal violence. Although my mother does all she can to keep it from me, I finally learn that Bella lives with a host family during the week, joining her mother and Rocco only on weekends. Rocco is gentle

60

and amiable, but regularly spouts bellicose anti-Arab rants that leave my mother mortified. She blushes and lowers her eyes, and her anger and shame burden me with a sort of ineffectual pity. It pains her to see me judging that repellent side of her Rocco's personality. But, I ask myself, why should I care? Why should I care, in the end, what becomes of her, so long as she's not being beaten? In his everyday behaviour, Rocco is a peaceable man. Of my two sisters she won't say a word, and no doubt she knows nothing. Losing custody of Bella during the week must have hurt her terribly. But in all her destitution she makes a great show of superiority and ebullience. I look at her, bewildered: can the fact that she's come to understand, as my father thought he'd realised many times, that she hasn't led a worthwhile life, and that her time on this earth will come to an end two or three decades hence, can that really explain such a renunciation of the woman she'd so stubbornly striven to become? All the same, I can only admire her bravado, however joyless. They're in difficult straits, forced to keep a careful eye on every meagre expense. Has she found work again? And Rocco, what does he do with his days? What of their income? She eludes my direct questions, gives me abstract answers – 'for as long as this world's been around, everything's always worked out in the end,' 'the job market is a snake that swallows its own tail,' 'we're holding our ground' – while, sheltered behind her enormous glasses, her eyes dart wildly this way and that, in search of a rescue she can't define.

The day I leave, I give her a green silk scarf. She immediately drapes it over her head, then changes her mind and wraps it oddly around her hips. I tell her about my children.

'Ah,' she says, deliberately cutting me off, 'aren't children the salt and pepper of our dull little lives?'

My mother is a woman in green, untouchable, disappointing, infinitely mutable, very cold, able, by force of will, to become very beautiful, and able, too, not to want to. Where are they now, my mother, Rocco, and Bella? I won't write to them and they won't write to me, until one day, perhaps, a letter might appear from some unknown place, accompanied by photos of unknown people who will happen to be my family, to various degrees – a letter whose authenticity, even if it's signed 'Maman,' I will dispute, and which I will then stuff away in some spot where it will never be unearthed again.

DECEMBER 2003 – The floodwaters now surround Katia Depetiteville's house. She's in no danger, but, isolated to a degree difficult to bear even for someone who lives in such solitude, she asks us on the phone to put her up for a while.

Jean-Yves hoists the rowboat onto the roof of the car, drives till the road disappears into the water, parks the car, takes the rowboat down from the roof, puts it in the water, and climbs in. The water has almost reached the threshold of Katia's house. Katia is waiting on the second floor, on her balcony, with a little pack on her back. Jean-Yves tells me all this later, staring at something invisible in the grey mist. With one single oar, he gently brought the rowboat under Katia's balcony, and then Katia straddled the balustrade and, without warning, threw herself off.

'Fortunately she landed in the rowboat,' says Jean-Yves, 'but she almost capsized us, and in any case, what was she trying to prove with an idiotic stunt like that?'

An absolute woman in green, Katia Depetiteville never shows any trace of gratitude for a favour that's been done her. Comfortably settled in with us, she exercises her rights as a houseguest with a voracity, almost a brutality, that I never see when I stop by her place for a cup of coffee, when the monotony of her life and the dreariness of her house so weigh on her that a gentle numbness is all she's capable of. Now she's come back to life, she speaks out, butts in with her opinions, lets herself be served and coddled. One day, she pulls on her green wool trousers and her bottle-green jumper and she and I set off for Bordeaux to catch the Paris train and pay a call on my two sisters, whose existence I suddenly recalled as I was reading a biography of the Papin sisters, and that memory of their obscure presence somewhere in the suburbs filled me with anxiety and contrition, making me think that although I could live perfectly well without seeing or thinking of them, it might perhaps be different for those two, who, apart from my now-exiled mother and indifferent father, have no other close relative than me. I scolded myself for rashly dismissing certain rumours concerning their dependence on alcohol and some sort of drug, respectively. And so I overcome my reticence, my repugnance for anything to do with my family. I fortify my resolve with Katia's company, Katia who's perfectly thrilled to be getting away from the Gironde, assuring me she hasn't been out of the region for a good twenty years, which I find doubtful, without saying so. I never point out Katia Depetiteville's flagrant inconsistencies to her face.

I struggle to remember the way to the building where, as the younger one told me this morning on the phone, my two sisters still live. Close beside me, Katia is gloomy and quiet – was she hoping for something a little more fun? Hoping this visit to the two girls was only a pretext for, once we reached Paris, going out on the town, seeing people? I don't know. I don't understand her. I really do not understand this Katia. But time has gone by, and my sisters look nothing like the girls they once were. Now they're two very heavy, very bulky women, who greet us with none of the awkwardness and timidity I recall from before. Their faces are pleasant, jovial, their eyes bright. Their beautiful black hair curls identically over their two pairs of shoulders. They're dressed in athletic wear of a fashionable style and brand, though it's entirely clear that neither of them practises any sport. Even I am surprised by the joy I feel on seeing them again. I embrace them one after the other, and under my fingers I can feel their bra straps digging into the abundant flesh on their backs. And then, from her sullen air, I deduce that Katia is disappointed by my very round, very substantial sisters, that she's already banished any impulse of sympathy or respect for them from her mind. She stands with her back pressed to the door, her arms crossed over her green jumper, her mouth disdainful, her green eyes motionless, distant. Angry, I whisper to her:

'No one's forcing you to stay, you know.'

Forever a woman in green in my memory, Katia Depetiteville opens the door behind her and backs out of the room with a wan smile on her lips. I never saw her again. I never heard anyone mention her again. Oh, she'll be back – but in what form? She'll be back – how can I know that?

My sisters have settled down now, their lives are almost established. The first one shows me a photograph of a young man with a brutish forehead: she'll be marrying him in a few weeks. Both of my sisters work, together, in some sort of government office. They inspire confidence, they're at peace – why is all of this nevertheless so sad? It's nothing more than life at its most ordinary – why is this all so sad? A wicked thought comes to me as I sip my tasteless tea, bored, in their little kitchen: it wasn't worth losing Katia Depetiteville just to come pay this charitable call on my sisters. Because I think of my mother, of Ivan's wife, of my stepmother, and I fear I'll see myself as a senseless fool should all those women in green disappear one by one, leaving me powerless to prove their existence, my own originality. I then wonder, in my sisters' tidy kitchen, how to find bearable a life without women in green exhibiting their slippery silhouettes in the background. In order to slip serenely through these moments of stupor, of deep boredom, of crippling inertia, I need to remember they decorate my thoughts, my invisible life, I need to remember they're there, at once real beings and literary figures, without which, it seems to me, the harshness of existence scours skin and flesh down to the bone.

'Did you go see Maman?' my younger sister asks, with that naive and unwavering kindliness I always find so moving.

'Did you go see Maman?' asks my other sister, more severely.

I tell them I saw our mother in Marseille, but they shake their heads with a 'tttss,' tell me they won't hear another word about that, and inform me that our mother is now once again living in this same building, on another floor, alone. She was lucky enough to get her old job back, in the neighbourhood school.

Disoriented, I ask:

'What about Bella? Where's her little girl?'

My sisters lower their eyelids, fringed with long, thick lashes. They hide their eyes, but I can see the inflexible creases of their mouths.

I stand up, mumble 'Goodbye,' and hurry out. An artificial scent of honeysuckle hangs in the air of their apartment, and my head is swimming. I'd seen more than one can of that freshener in every room, and three or four times in the course of my stay I saw one or the other of my sisters go and reflexively press the button to fill the air with perfume.

I start downstairs, gripping the banister. I reach the landing on my mother's floor and go to her door, pressing one ear against it, and from the other side I hear the regular sound of deep breathing, as if my mother were sitting on a chair with her own ear glued to the door, waiting, inert, perhaps lulled to sleep by the rhythm of her own breathing, so heavy, so masculine. I feel anger and pity. A little later, as I was nearing the ground floor, I thought my mother's door had swung open. Maybe she saw me, maybe she called out to me – maybe not.

That same year, determined to put my affection for my father to the test, I accept an invitation from a Cultural Centre in Ouagadougou to take part in a literary symposium, knowing that my father and his wife, who've left Paris and the seed shop, now live in that part of the world – although I can't be sure it's the same wife, my one-time friend, since, out of vanity, boredom, and restlessness, my father has never let his marriages last. Whatever I find there, I tell myself, and whoever this person is whose life he's now sharing, in his inability to be alone, whatever I find there, I tell myself, I'll pass no judgement, I'll inflict no acidic or severe or sarcastic gaze on this probable new couple. I'm going to see him because he won't come and see me, and my solicitude for him, my devotion, all those tender feelings, however tinged with regret, couldn't bear for long the distance between us, couldn't bear for long the years going by without seeing or speaking to each other. He doesn't know me all that well, never having lived with me, and I think he forgets about me when he doesn't have my face before his eyes to remind him of the girl he one day engendered. And besides, this man, my father, this anxious, intelligent, disturbingly thin man, prides himself on never opening a novel, so I know he hasn't read my work, I know he'd rather have no notion of the reality of my books' existence, out of respect for me in a sense, since he considers literature so ignoble a thing. All of that I can put up with today, all of that has ceased to anger me, all of that might almost strike me as funny, and in any case I no longer seize on it as grounds for recrimination. Why take it amiss? I ask myself. Isn't it actually better this way, isn't it best that parents not read their children's novels? What might they find there that could possibly be good for them?

And so, invited by the Cultural Centre and not by my father, I get on the plane for Ouagadougou with my oldest daughter Marie, who's eleven. We're met at the airport by the centre's secretary, a certain Monsieur Urbain, who already seems to know everything there is to know about us. Straight off, he asks:

'And will your father be at your talk?'

'He doesn't know I'm here,' I say.

'Oh, of course he does, I beg your pardon,' says Monsieur Urbain.

'I hope he won't come to the talk,' I say somewhat curtly.

I want Monsieur Urbain to understand that it would be a good idea to dissuade my father from attending the symposium.

'That's not his world, and he wouldn't be comfortable,' says Marie.

'He looks on literature with loathing and contempt, you understand,' I add.

Whereupon Monsieur Urbain wraps himself in a mildly irked silence, as if he were the subject of this conversation, as if my father, disguised as Monsieur Urbain, were showing his irritation at being described in this way. But I know well that my father wouldn't be offended at all, that he'd be proud to hear himself spoken of as an enemy of novelists, for in his eyes literature is a failing. That's why he heaps mocking disdain on men who write, men more than women, who can in fact, he believes, bear that stigma with a certain glamour, so long as they're pretty. That's how my father is – my father, whom, it's very clear, you will never, by word or by deed, succeed in convincing of anything whatsoever. You can curse him, call down every possible disaster upon him, and then, without his noticing, without his even being able to imagine such a thing, find yourself forgiving him, if only so as to be humiliated no more by that needling, pointless exasperation, by that petulant, impotent rage. That's how my father is, I then think to myself, light-heartedly. And this is how Monsieur Urbain is, who, forgetting his duties as a host, clings to his vexed silence as we drive down the narrow rutted road towards the Cultural Centre. At one point, though, he turns towards us and points at a large pink stucco building, brand-new, separated from the road by an iron fence with spikes on the bars.

'That's my house,' he says, 'and it was your father,' he adds proudly, as if taking some obscure sort of revenge (but is he avenging fathers, Africans, disparagers of literature?) 'it was your father who designed it.'

Marie and I can't help laughing, amiably, but surely with a hint of involuntary savagery, as well.

'I'm sorry, we're clearly not talking about the same person,' I say. 'Whomever you're thinking of, he can't possibly be my father. My father is not an architect.'

But even as I speak these words, a hesitation, an uncertainty turns my gaze away from Monsieur Urbain's nape. I begin to doubt my own objections. I ask:

'Really, my father's an architect? I didn't know.'

Then, vaguely, a very distant time comes into my memory, a time when, as a child, I might possibly have heard my father alluding to construction problems, intractable difficulties of design. Unless, I tell myself, I'm making that memory up and don't even know it, unsettled as I am by Monsieur Urbain's claims.

'Your poor father,' he says simply, by way of an answer.

Still fearing he might appear in the lecture hall, not wanting him to hear me speak, or to unleash a barrage of humiliating, naively belligerent questions that would only reveal the depth of his cultural ignorance and bad faith, Marie and I hire a cab to pay a call at my father's house that very night. He lives in the outskirts of Ouagadougou, and I'm surprised to find myself being driven through a sort of tangled, ramshackle suburb, not at all the kind of genteel neighbourhood he always chose to settle in. All the same, the house we pull up to is presentable, moderately large, its stucco in need of repair. A woman is sitting in the fading light of the yard. She's my stepmother, the one I know from before, who was my great friend as a teenager. Her ample body is wrapped in a green and black boubou. She's staring at the ground between her wide-spread legs, hands flat on her knees, still and enigmatically idle, but on seeing us she immediately sits up and comes scurrying to meet me. She clasps me to her bosom, and I feel as though I were rediscovering the softness and sweet scent of her high-school girl neck, that slightly insistent way of pressing her cheek against mine before planting the ritual kiss. Moved, I begin to wonder if it really was to see my father, and not my stepmother, that I came all this way – and then back comes the tinge of sadness that's always veiled my thoughts about her, linked to the certainty that she abandoned her vocation, her free will, her joyousness, just to become one with this man, my father, whose life was nothing more than a long string of disenchantments, who appeared before her, my slightly gullible friend, in a beguiling aura of counterfeit ebullience, my fatuous father, so taken with himself, so jealously protective of his thinness, so little able to succeed in anything whatsoever.

Clasped in my stepmother's arms, I don't dare whisper in her ear: 'Don't you want to come away with us? Leave him, come on, leave him!'

Because, ever since her marriage, she's no longer my friend and my equal. She belongs to the generation before me. And besides, do I really have the right to take such measures for the purpose of hurting my father? Why hurt him, when I've come here for no other reason than to show him my affection? I'm free to forget or neglect him, if I like, I'm free to consider him dead – why come here and try to do him harm? He married my friend, but that's no reason, I tell myself, to want to punish him.

A little later, my father appears. And all those bad thoughts I was thinking, all my dreams of confiscating his wife, I choke them all back and renounce them, the moment I see my father feeling his way along the walls and realise he's now almost blind. He pretends there's nothing wrong, and welcomes us into his home as if he could actually see us. A kind of dull-white film on his corneas leaves his gaze opaque and empty.

'It's cataracts,' my stepmother tells me later, with a fatalistic shrug.

And when I talk about an operation, she says it's too late now.

'We would have had to go back to France when it first started,' she says. 'We couldn't, we didn't have the money. That's how it is.'

Another shrug, resigned and indifferent, her brown eyes almost as dull as my father's. She takes next to no notice of Marie. And I'm disappointed that my father can't make out Marie's features, having secretly hoped that, finding her so perfectly loveable, he might regret not having raised any of his own daughters, and that this regret might be for him a suffering, an affliction, a thorn lodged in the hide of his egotism. But no, nothing of the sort – to be sure, why come here only to hurt him, but really, what's the good of coming here only to find nothing and no one in any way changed by my coming? Saying hello to Marie, he pretends to be speaking to her, but it is to a shape with no face and no clear outline that he tosses out two or three formal sentences, in a voice that, given the circumstances, can hardly be full of warmth.

'I hear you've gone in for architecture,' I say.

'I designed two or three beautiful houses. But that's all over now, I got sick of it.'

I will next ask my stepmother:

'Why won't he admit he can't see?'

'He's embarrassed,' she tells me, with the cold indolence that is now hers.

Marie and I are invited to stay for dinner at my father's. Emerging from various rooms of the house, three or four young men sit down at the table beside us, all of them my father's children, but all born to different women, none of whom I know. They're uncomfortable, grim, unsmiling. The house's dejected atmosphere ends up affecting Marie, who came here so full of sentimental dreams of a reunion, and I see her bury her nose in her plate, of interest to no one, diluted in the flood of descendents.

My father holds forth. He pretends to turn his glassy gaze towards each of us in turn. We're served nothing but a single dish of semolina with vegetable broth, garnished with a small helping of chickpeas. They have no money, I tell myself. They're stuck here in Burkina, in a neighbourhood my proud father would once never even have deigned to drive through, because they have no money and nowhere to go, in spite of my father's many children on three continents.

And all alone my father talks on, joyless, practised. He's wearing a Western suit, well-tailored but not particularly clean. Around him, his children are downcast.

Should I rescue my father and stepmother? Should I help them come back to France? And what will they do then? I deeply regret having come here, and I don't know what to think of this man. I believe I can glimpse one impervious part of him, one sole part unchanged over decades of a disorderly life, which shelters his exclusive love for himself. I don't know what to think of him. I find him smug and unsympathetic. Can I rescue my father? Can I even offer my aid to this man who always made it a point of honour to put up a prosperous front? And how can I even think of taking on two supplementary souls, my father and my stepmother, so ill-equipped, how can I think of bringing them into my house, of living with them, even temporarily? Would she then cease to be my stepmother and become my dearest friend once again? And those adult children, anxious and sullen, who my father houses under his roof, what would become of them?

My stepmother chews slowly, staring into the distance. My father pontificates, to the indifference of all, and now he's moved on to Monsieur Urbain – that bastard, as he calls him – and his house.

'This Urbain thinks very highly of you,' I say, overcome with pity for my father.

'If I dared,' he says, 'I'd blow up that house of his, and him along with it.'

'The beautiful house you designed?'

'Yes,' says my father. 'The hell with art. The bastard never paid me.'

My father then flies into a terrifying rage. His tone stays steady, but his hands shake, his thighs twitch under the table, his entire face is convulsed by tics. The young men who surround him, his late-life offspring, glum and downhearted, the wretched children of his middle age, his bitter age, are staring at the table, slightly hunched in their chairs, as if long accustomed, I tell myself, to taking these defensive measures when the tempest starts to rage. I've spent little time in the company of my father, but I've always heard, and always seen for myself, that he was a gentle man – stubborn but peaceable, unconciliatory but clement. And here I see violence radiating from his whole skeletal body. He leaps to his feet, toppling his chair.

'If it was just him, that would be one thing,' he says in his flat voice. 'But the others are just as bad, they never paid me either. That's why we live this way, you understand?'

He picks up his plateful of semolina and chickpeas. He throws it through the open window. We hear the plate break in the courtyard. Dumbstruck, Marie lets out a shocked little giggle.

'He does that at almost every meal,' my stepmother whispers. 'It's only an act, just a new way he's found to keep himself from eating.'

I ask:

'Is it true no one's paid him?'

'I think it's only right,' she says. 'They pretend to believe he's an architect, or at least a competent architect, and he pretends to design houses, I mean he draws up blueprints but they don't make any sense, and then when it's all done they pretend to pay him. It's not for real, no one thinks it's for real. But now your father pretends to believe it's for real, and after all that time pretending maybe he thinks it's the truth. Oh, don't ask me. I'm so sick of it all, so sick of it all,' my stepmother adds, with a sort of weary intensity.

There's nothing left in her of the girl she used to be – and what about me? I'd have to ask her to find out, but does she remember our friendship, who we were? I'm not sure she does. Through clenched jaws, her teeth bitterly gnashing, she tells me she's come up with all sorts of projects since she got to Burkina, but thanks to my father – unhelpful, jealous, sometimes poisonously disloyal – they've all come to nothing.

'Oh, I can't stand it anymore,' says my stepmother. 'I mean it, I'm tired, tired, I don't care what happens next. I have no children, I have nothing. He's got too many children, and I don't have any. Now I don't care anymore.'

Evidently my father has resolved to let himself waste away. He pretends to eat, but actually swallows only a few spoonfuls of semolina every day. So my stepmother tells me, in her cold despair. What can I do? They all need saving – the two of them, the young men in their clutches – but who's supposed to do it? I wish I hadn't come here, and hadn't learned of, hadn't witnessed such a disaster. I also wish Marie had never witnessed or learned of this ugly, glacial ruin, the fruit of my father's vanity. Marie is a young French girl of her time: understandably, she was hoping for warm feelings and sensitivity. And now she's discovering an incomprehensible paralysis of the sentiments, a collective indifference and sabotage: the slow agony of a household revolving around a master whose taste for death is no longer kept under wraps.

The next day, the lecture hall is half empty. At the very back, I can see my stepmother, fortunately alone. She's chatting with Marie, and she sends me a cheerful little wave that warms my heart. And two days later, she's the one who comes to say goodbye to us at the airport, again alone.

'I'm going to do whatever it takes to get back to France, as soon as I possibly can,' she says. 'If your father wants to stay, he can stay.'

I look at her round face, her eyes, wildly aglow with a hope I can't quite define.

'And what about him, what'll happen to him?' asks Marie.

'He's on his way to an early grave,' says my step- mother, defeated.

She then informs me that, having no family left to come home to, when she gets to France she'll stay with my own mother while she looks for a new job and apartment. I thought my friend had completely lost touch with my mother since our high-school years: I didn't realise they've been writing since the days of the Ledada, regularly exchanging photos and news, in the name of a fidelity to the past and to my father that I have some difficulty understanding. She's kept up with all my mother's adventures in Marseille, and so, a little dazed by the oddity of the situation, I ask her:

'Whatever became of the little girl? Bella?'

She tells me that Bella stayed behind in Marseille, with a foster family, that my mother goes down to see her twice a month, that she – my friend, that is – hope to make the trip with my mother one day, and make Bella's acquaintance.

'But still… What's going to happen to him, all alone here?' Marie asks again.

'You can't go on loving someone who won't eat,' my stepmother says, matter-of-factly.

We hugged her, then hugged her again, and we walked off towards the departure lounge, looking back over our shoulders now and then to see her petrified silhouette growing smaller and smaller, standing stock still on the concourse, as if she had only to stay there unmoving for a few days or weeks to finally end up on an airplane, all her problems miraculously solved behind her back, by the sheer force of her mineral inertia.

I still don't know if my friend, if my stepmother has come back to France, and I don't know who's putting her up. I dream that one morning, perhaps, in fifteen years, or twenty, I'll hear the little bell on my gate ringing, and before me I'll see a small dark-haired girl who'll say to me: 'I'm your half-sister Bella,' in a timid, tremulous voice, with an echo of something green in it – just as her eyes will be green, and green her jumper and her trousers, so that none of this ever comes to an end.

Hearing shouts, I leaned out of the window, and in the middle of the street I saw a circle of children pressed close together, bending down, gathered around something or someone. I tried to make out what it might be, but in vain. I looked again, alarmed, and thought I saw two of my own children among them. What were they doing there, absorbed and thoughtful, sometimes letting out little cries and warnings? What were they doing there, hiding their faces and blocking the street?

Between their legs I saw a dark form, moving and anxious.

I bolt out of the room, race down the big staircase. My bare feet slap loudly against the wood. I say to myself, and say again, frantic: I'll never make it in time. And then again: Please God, let me make it in time. The steps seem to be multiplying diabolically, I feel like I'll never get to the bottom. Down and down I run, never reaching the landing, while, from the street, I hear the children's voices, ever more excited, unbridled.

I lay my hands on my children's shoulders, as gently as possible.

'What's going on here? Time to come in now,' I say.

'It ran away!'

'It was all black! It ran off, it's quick!'

The children ask if I saw it, if I can tell them the name of what I saw. They turn their bewitched little faces towards mine. Some of them seem sated, exhausted, like lion cubs after a feast.

'Time to come in now,' I say, shivering. 'No, I don't know what that's called,' I tell them. 'I don't think it has a name in our language.'

Since they say nothing, I add:

'To tell you the truth, I didn't see anything. Nothing at all. What was it?'

Then the children eye each other gravely. Their lips are very red. Then they look away, and fall silent.

December 2003 – The water's stopped rising. But in La Réole the riverside streets are submerged, and the ground floors of the modest houses are flooded. Above them, on the bridge, the passers-by stand motionless, looking at the water, waiting for nothing more, only the simple spectacle of water where it's not supposed to be.

And then... driving slowly across the flooded plain, on the one passable road... I wonder... the water muddy and calm on either side of the roadway... is the Garonne... is the Garonne a woman in green?

MARIE NDIAYE met her father for the first time at age fifteen, two years before publishing her first novel. She is the recipient of the Prix Femina and the Prix Goncourt, the latter being the highest honour a French writer can receive. One of ten finalists for the 2013 Man Booker International Prize, alongside Lydia Davis and Marilynne Robinson, she is the author of over a dozen plays and works of prose.

JORDAN STUMP is one of the leading translators of innovative French literature. The recipient of numerous honours and prizes, he has translated books by Nobel laureate Claude Simon, Jean-Philippe Toussaint, and Éric Chevillard, as well as Jules Verne's French-language novel *The Mysterious Island*. His translation of Marie NDiaye's *All My Friends* was shortlisted for the French-American Foundation Translation Prize.

Influx Press is an independent publisher based in London, committed to publishing innovative and challenging literature from across the UK and beyond.

Lifetime supporters: Bob West and Barbara Richards

www.influxpress.com
@Influxpress